# The Awesome Autistic
# Guide for Trans Teens

*by the same author*

**The Autism and Neurodiversity Self Advocacy Handbook**
**Developing the Skills to Determine Your Own Future**
*Barb Cook and Yenn Purkis*
ISBN 978 1 78775 575 8
eISBN 978 1 78775 576 5

**The Autistic Trans Guide to Life**
*Yenn Purkis and Wenn Lawson*
*Foreword by Dr Emma Goodall*
ISBN 978 1 78775 391 4
eISBN 978 1 78775 392 1

**The Awesome Autistic Go-To Guide**
**A Practical Handbook for Autistic Teens and Tweens**
*Yenn Purkis and Tanya Masterman*
*Illustrated by Glynn Masterman*
Foreword by Dr Emma Goodall
ISBN 978 1 78775 316 7
eISBN 978 1 78775 317 4

*of related interest*

**Queerly Autistic**
**The Ultimate Guide for LGBTQIA+ Teens on the Spectrum**
*Erin Ekins*
ISBN 978 1 78775 171 2
eISBN 978 1 78775 172 9

**The Spectrum Girl's Survival Guide**
**How to Grow Up Awesome and Autistic**
*Siena Castellon*
*Foreword by Temple Grandin*
ISBN 978 1 78775 183 5
eISBN 978 1 78775 184 2

# THE AWESOME AUTISTIC GUIDE FOR TRANS TEENS

**Yenn Purkis** and **Sam Rose**

Illustrated by Glynn Masterman

**Jessica Kingsley Publishers**
London and Philadelphia

First published in Great Britain in 2022 by Jessica Kingsley Publishers
An imprint of Hodder & Stoughton Ltd
An Hachette Company

1

**Disclaimer:** The information contained in this book is not intended
to replace the services of trained medical professionals or to be a
substitute for medical advice. You are advised to consult a doctor
on any matters relating to your health, and in particular on any
matters that may require diagnosis or medical attention.

A CIP catalogue record for this title is available from
the British Library and the Library of Congress

ISBN 978 1 83997 076 4
eISBN 978 1 83997 077 1

Printed and bound in Great Britain by Clays Ltd

Jessica Kingsley Publishers' policy is to use papers that are natural,
renewable and recyclable products and made from wood grown in
sustainable forests. The logging and manufacturing processes are expected
to conform to the environmental regulations of the country of origin.

Jessica Kingsley Publishers
Carmelite House
50 Victoria Embankment
London EC4Y 0DZ

www.jkp.com

# Contents

# Introduction

Hi readers! Welcome to this book. The authors are Sam and Yenn. We are both autistic and gender divergent, which is a good thing because this book is all about being autistic and gender divergent. We would like to introduce ourselves before we get into the book.

## YENN

I am Yenn. I was diagnosed as autistic when I was 20, way back in 1994. Back then there was not a lot of understanding of what autism is, and life was very hard. I struggled to live my life and ended up in lots of very scary situations. I am also non-binary. This means that my gender is neither male nor female but a sort of third option. While I have been non-binary all my life, I didn't understand this about myself until I was 43! This is because when I was younger there was not a lot of understanding around gender diversity. I am very proud to be autistic, and I am very proud to be non-binary. Autism and gender divergence form a big part of my identity and what makes me me. I am also an autism advocate. This means that I support autistic people, mostly through writing and giving presentations. I hope that this book will give you the skills and tools to manage your lives well and be proud of who you are.

# SAM

I am Sam. I realized that I was autistic at university, and after reading about it online and meeting other autistic people, I sought a diagnosis a year later. A couple of years after that I realized that another word that explained how I thought and felt was 'transgender'. Nowadays, I mostly label myself as genderqueer, trans or trans-masculine, or non-binary, but I do find that there are many other labels that fit me too. I love to read and learn about autism and other types of brains, and I want to use what I learn to help the community. I studied psychology at university where I learnt about how different brains work and how to look after your mental wellbeing. It took me a while to learn how to manage my own brain, but I am glad that I did, because now I can enjoy the world much more than

I ever expected. There is a lot of beauty out there to be explored and shared, and we need all kinds of brains to do it.

## Why did we write this book?

When we were young, there was not a lot of information out there for trans and gender-diverse autistic young people. In fact, there still isn't! This means that trans and gender-diverse autistic young people can feel quite alone and not know what to do. This book is all about helping you, the reader, to understand yourself in terms of your identity as an autistic person and as a trans person. It has tips and strategies to help you manage life well. This book is all about inclusion and respect and about being proud of who you are. It is also about understanding and knowing that you are awesome, just as you are.

We would absolutely have loved to have had this book when we were growing up. We didn't have it, of course, because it wasn't written, but you have it and that is a great thing! We hope it will be really helpful. This book is all for you: for autistic and gender-diverse young people. It is written for you by two autistic and gender-divergent people. We really hope you like it and get a lot of useful information and tips from it. Welcome to *The Awesome Autistic Guide for Trans Teens*.

## Chapter 1

# All About Autism and Gender Diversity

# WHAT IS AUTISM?

Autism is a difference in the way some people's brains are wired. It usually results in people viewing the world differently and having a range of different experiences from most people. Autism is a *difference* rather than a disease or deficit. It does not make people less important or valuable than others and it does not mean a person is broken and needs fixing. Despite this fact, autistic people can have a difficult time in life. There are ways to help address this, and most of them involve helping non-autistic people to understand autism better.

# AUTISM AND LANGUAGE

There are many words used to describe autism and autistic people. Some of these are positive and respectful and others aren't. In terms of talking about being autistic, there are a few options. One is 'I have autism.' Another is 'I am on the spectrum', and another is 'I am autistic.' Ways of talking about your autism are sometimes called ways of 'identifying'. Different people identify in different ways. A lot of people say 'I am autistic' because they feel it is more inclusive. Autism is an important part of who a person is, so saying 'I have autism' doesn't really reflect that very well. The authors of this book use 'I am autistic' – also known as identity-first language – as we feel that autism is a key part of what makes us who we are. However, whichever way you choose to identify is right for you. You can't tell a person that the way they are identifying is wrong. In terms of talking about people who are not autistic, we use the word 'neurotypical'. This describes a person who is not autistic and not neurodivergent in any other way. (Neurodivergent means having one or more conditions such as autism, ADD/ADHD, dyslexia, Tourette's or dyspraxia, to name a few. Autistic people often have additional neurodivergent conditions.) If a person is neurodivergent but not autistic, then 'non-autistic' is a good way to describe them, as they are neurodivergent but not autistic.

## CHARACTERISTICS OF AUTISM

Some of the experiences that are common to young people who are autistic include:

- Having passionate interests – sometimes called 'obsessions' or 'special interests'. Basically, this means having an intense love of a topic or fandom

- Heightened sensory experiences including smell, taste, sound, vision and touch

- Ability to focus closely on a topic

- Being able to pick up on the feelings of others even if you can't see outward expressions such as crying

- Feeling emotions differently to others, sometimes very strongly or sometimes not at all

- Logical approach to life

- Anxiety

- More likely to be trans and gender divergent

- Honesty

- Love for animals

- Literal interpretation of conversations

- Being very thoughtful

- Creativity

- Being gifted

- Experiencing overload and meltdowns and shutdowns

- Struggling to read facial expressions

- Struggling to recognize faces, sometimes even those of family members

- Getting along well with other autistic and/or neurodivergent people

- Having friends who are significantly older or younger than you.

It is important to be aware that all autistic people are different and will experience the world in different ways. This list of autistic characteristics will not be true for some autistic people, and some autistic people will have all of these characteristics. Autism is experienced differently by every single autistic person, so this list is a guide of things you might experience. But don't worry if you do not have all or any of the criteria on the list! Some of the characteristics of autism are positive and others are not. Other characteristics are neither good nor bad and some are good for one person but not for another.

## ACTIVITY: If you can, list three things you like about yourself

1. ............................................

2. ............................................

3. ............................................

# IS THERE 'MALE' AND 'FEMALE' AUTISM?

Some people talk about autism and autistic characteristics as being 'male' or 'female'. This involves separating the characteristics of autism into 'male' or 'female' types. While this might seem logical at first, in actual fact it is not a very sensible or accurate way of looking at autism. You can find lists of these gender-based characteristics online and in books, but they don't really represent reality for many autistic people.

The first issue with male and female types is that they simply aren't correct. Autistic boys can have 'female' characteristics and autistic girls can have the 'male' characteristics. But it is actually more problematic than that. This book, as the title suggests, is all about autism and gender diversity. A *lot* of autistic people – kids, young people and adults – are trans and gender divergent. There is no list of transgender autistic characteristics. This means that putting gender-based labels on autistic people misses all of the trans and gender-divergent autistic people.

Put simply, autism is autism. Autistic people, be they female, male, cisgender, non-binary or trans, are all different. The characteristics and personalities of autistic people are as varied as all the many hundreds of thousands of autistic people are themselves. It is misleading and confusing to talk about male or female autism.

## CAMOUFLAGING/'MASKING'

Many autistic people do something called masking or camouflaging. This means acting differently to their true selves when in social situations, particularly social situations with neurotypical people.

All people will struggle to be their most intimate selves in public. This means that most people develop a sort of armour to wear out in the social world. Everyone does this, but it is even more true for people who are already 'more different', like autistic people. People who are not autistic and whose brains are wired for being social can be seen to have a more herd-like mentality. That is, they may recognize social norms easily and fit into the social world really well. Autistic people are less likely to have brains wired in a way that allows them to be easily social when with others. Therefore, autistic people may feel they need to camouflage and not be their true selves if they want to be socially accepted. This doesn't mean the person is lying or trying to trick others. It is more a survival tactic to enable autistic people to be accepted in a social world where people often do not accept us. Camouflaging can be very draining and can contribute to overload and meltdowns and shutdowns. It would be nice if we did not need to camouflage due to autistic people being accepted in the neurotypical world, but sadly this is often not the case.

## WHAT IS GENDER DIVERSITY?

Gender diversity is the concept that everyone has a different gender identity. Gender diversity means that there are many more than two genders in the world. Anyone who feels outside of the two genders we have in Western culture is *gender divergent*, meaning our gender identities don't follow the same path as what is expected for males or females. There are probably as many gender identities as there are people on this planet. Our sense of our gender can be a deeply held and very personal thing.

Male and female can be seen as binary genders, but they are far from the only genders. Here are some terms around gender that are helpful to know. These are:

- **Trans and gender divergent people** – people who do not identify as the sex they were assigned at birth. There is a large number of trans and gender-divergent identities, which we will talk about in greater detail later in this book.

- **Cisgender** – this simply means a person who identifies as the sex they were assigned at birth. It is from a Latin word meaning 'on the same side as'. It is not an insult.

- **Trans/transgender** – a person who does not identify with the sex they were assigned at birth. Transgender people can identify as male or female or something else.

- **Non-binary** – non-binary people do not identify as binary male or female. There are a lot of different non-binary identities, which we will look at later in this book.

- **Transphobia** – transphobia is hatred, bigotry or trolling against trans and gender-divergent people.

- **Trans man/trans-masculine** – a trans man or a trans-masculine person is a transgender person who transitions from female to male and identifies as male and/or masculine.

- **Trans woman/trans-feminine** – a trans woman or a trans-feminine person is a transgender person who transitions from male to female and identifies as female and/or feminine.

- **Gender dysphoria** – gender dysphoria means a person feels distressed and uncomfortable with the gender they were assigned at birth. Many but not all transgender people experience gender dysphoria.

## WHY IT IS GOOD TO BE GENDER DIVERGENT

Some people are bigoted about gender diversity and will bully or attack trans and gender-divergent people. This can make people feel as if they don't want to be transgender or as if there is something wrong with them. But in reality, being trans and gender divergent can be a great thing. You do not choose your gender. It is part of who you are that you cannot change. So, embracing it and feeling proud of who you are is also a great thing. You are yourself, and you are awesome just the way you are. If a person has a problem with you and your gender identity, then it is definitely their problem, not yours! This book will help you to understand who you are and help you to be proud of yourself. Gender diversity is a natural part of being human, and trans and gender-divergent people have a lot to offer and contribute. You have the right to be treated with respect, and you have the right to be yourself.

# ⇒ Chapter 2 ⇐

# All About Being Gender Diverse

# YOU ARE NOT ALONE

As you read in Chapter 1, trans and gender-divergent identities make up a big part of gender diversity; we are found all over the world! Autistic people can also be trans or gender divergent. In fact, there seems to be quite a lot of gender diversity in the autistic community. Some research suggests that autistic people are seven times more likely to be trans or gender divergent than non-autistic people! You are unique, but you are definitely not alone.

In some countries, there is a lot of progress being made to better support and respect gender diversity. You may have heard of the 'Progress Pride Flag', which has striped rainbow colours as well as an arrow of black, brown, blue, pink and white stripes on the left. This flag was created to recognize the hard work of transgender people of colour such as Marsha P. Johnson, who fought for our right to freely express our gender identities without shame or fear. Sadly, this isn't true everywhere in the world yet, and many people struggle to come out safely to their family, to their community, or even in their own country.

For those who live in more accepting places, this progress means that there is a growing understanding of how to best support gender-divergent teens. There should be plenty of services and resources available to help you learn about and share your identity safely. The same goes for autism too; as autism becomes better understood, you will have more freedom to learn about and get the support that best suits you. Young people especially need these things because the teenage years are an important time for learning about yourself and developing your own sense of identity.

There are many spaces that can help connect you up to other people who are autistic and trans. There may be a Pride group at your school or in your local community. If there isn't something available in your area now, there might be one on its way, or perhaps you could even start one of your own! Author Sam runs an online group for autistic LGBTQIA+ teenagers, so they get to hang out with other trans autistics every week. Before this, Sam wasn't sure how many other people felt similarly to them. Now they know that plenty of others are out there too.

Even if you don't know anyone personally, trust that there are many other autistic people out there who feel similarly to you.

# ACTIVITY: List some organizations that provide advocacy or support for LGBTQIA+ young people in your local area

If you can't think of any, would you consider starting your own?

1. ...........................................

2. ...........................................

3. ...........................................

# HOW DO YOU KNOW YOU ARE GENDER DIVERGENT?

Gender can be viewed as a *social construction*. This means that gender is an idea created by humans as a way to better understand the world and the people in it. Gender is an idea that has been developed over thousands of years across all cultures. Because gender is a social construction, it means that it is a work in progress, and the more we learn about people's experiences of gender, the better we can find new words to express ourselves authentically.

You may have heard the term 'gender diverse', but have you heard the term 'gender divergent'? These terms might sound similar, but their meanings are quite different: diversity is a characteristic of a group, while divergence is a characteristic of an individual. For example, Sam is gender *divergent* because they are non-binary, but their football team is gender *diverse* because it has a range of gender identities within it.

The whole world is gender diverse because it takes all kinds of genders to create gender diversity. The same way there needs to be lots of different animals, plants and fungi to create biodiversity, there needs to be lots of different genders to create gender diversity!

Someone whose gender fits outside of what labels our culture hands down will be considered gender divergent. In Western culture, only two genders have traditionally been recognized. This is what is called the 'gender binary', which is centred around being a man/boy or being a woman/girl. Because Western culture has a huge influence over the rest of the world's cultures, the gender binary is sometimes assumed to be the *only* way to think about gender, though this is not true. The idea of gender is completely different in different cultures; there might be three, four, or more gender identities in some societies. For example, two-spirit people are a third gender identity in Indigenous North American cultures, and the Bugis people from an area of Indonesia recognize five distinct gender identities!

If you are gender divergent, it generally means that you feel outside of the Western binary of man or woman, boy or girl. If the label you were assigned at birth doesn't feel quite right on you, you might want to explore this further, or you may have already found something that fits better. It could mean that you use a gender label that is completely different to what was assigned to you or that you keep the assigned label but don't feel very attached to it.

We like to think about gender similarly to how we think about genres of music. Saying there are only two genders, boy and girl, is like saying there are only two kinds of songs: rap and classical. In reality, there are many different kinds of songs, and we can classify them into many different kinds of genres. Some songs fit many genres and some fit none. This idea is the same for gender too. There are many different kinds of people, and we can classify ourselves into many different genders. You cannot choose your gender identity, but you can choose how you want to express that identity. It all comes down to how you think about your gender and how you want to share that part of yourself with the world.

Some people know from a really young age that they don't identify with the gender they were assigned at birth. Other people might not realize this feeling until they are much older. Regardless of how old you are, it can be really scary trying to figure out if you are gender divergent, but the trick is not to overthink it. It is OK to be gender divergent, and it is OK not to be. As you have read above, gender is a pretty fuzzy idea anyway, and our understanding of it develops as we grow, both as individuals and as a society. There are many different ways you can think about and express your gender, and if there's some way that you want to express yourself, there's no harm in giving it a go and seeing how you feel. That might look like wearing some new style of clothing or trying a new name or pronoun, even if it is just around your home. See how it makes you feel. If it makes you feel good, then you may have found out some more about your gender identity!

If you are having trouble understanding what your thoughts and feelings mean, it might be useful to try out some different ways of communicating them to yourself or to others. If you can't tell what emotion you are experiencing, but you want to know more about it, here are some different ways that might work for you:

- Writing in a diary or writing a letter. You could write to yourself or others

- Drawing or painting. You could think about the colours, lines, characters or whatever you choose to draw and see whether they help make any thoughts or feelings clearer

- Writing poetry or a song about your feelings

- Playing an instrument

- Finding art or music that you like and thinking about what feelings or thoughts they are about

- Talking it through with trusted family, friends or a counsellor

- Being around people who are important to you. Sometimes you don't need to say anything to communicate; just spending time with others might allow you to think things through better than if you are alone.

# WHAT ARE SOME DIFFERENT GENDER IDENTITIES?

A good way to think about gender identities is through the genderbread person. The genderbread person looks at gender identity, gender expression, anatomical sex, and sexual and romantic attraction. The genderbread person infographic can be found at genderbread.org. This can be a helpful resource for understanding how gender can vary across individuals but also how you think of your own gender.

There are so many different gender identities that it can sometimes feel a bit overwhelming. Just remember that everyone's sense of gender is unique and that gender-identity labels are words that we share to try to capture overlapping parts of that experience.

If you are not sure which label fits you best, that is totally fine. You can choose not to use labels or you can choose multiple labels. You might find that the labels you use change over time or based on how you are feeling. Sam finds that there are many gender-identity labels that they align themselves with, but mostly they just say that they are non-binary. Having said that, many people identify strongly with a particular gender identity, and it can be a great way for someone to connect with themselves and others who feel similarly.

Here are just a few gender-identity labels:

- **Agender** – you do not feel like gender is a strong part of your identity, or you do not identify with the concept of gender at all.

- **Autigender** – your gender identity is strongly related to your autistic identity. Autism is a neurotype, and some people feel that this has shaped their gender identity so much that they are hard to separate. Only autistic people can identify as autigender.

- **Brotherboy/sistergirl** – these are transgender identities exclusive to First Nations cultures in Australia. A brotherboy is a transgender male, and a sistergirl is a transgender female. Many indigenous cultures across the world have their own trans and non-binary gender identities.

- **Demigender** – people who are demigender feel a little bit, but not fully, like one of binary genders of male and female. For example, someone who is a demiboy might feel a little like a boy, but not fully. A demigirl will feel a little like a girl, but not fully. You could put the prefix demi- in front of any other gender-identity label if you feel a bit like it, e.g. demi-agender, demi-genderfluid.

- **Genderfluid** – your gender identity changes regularly. It could change between binary identities or between any range of other gender identities.

- **Non-binary** – you don't identify as simply 'male' or 'female'; you identify somewhere in between these two, somewhere else completely or nowhere.

- **Transgender** – this means you identify as a gender that is different from the one you were assigned at birth.

If none of what we have written above seems to fit your own sense of gender, there are many more labels out there to explore.

# WHAT IS PRIDE?

Pride means to feel proud about who you are. Pride means that you aren't ashamed about being trans, or autistic, or anything else that is part of your identity. The idea of Pride for the queer community was started in 1970 by a bisexual woman named Brenda Howard. Brenda Howard organized the first Pride parade, after the 1969 Stonewall Riots, where transgender people stood up for their equal rights in society. Brenda Howard helped create this movement as a way to celebrate the importance of the LGBTQIA+ community feeling pride and to raise awareness of inequalities that LGBTQIA+ people still experience. Nowadays, Pride parades are held all over the world in June, which is the official Pride Month.

There is also Autistic Pride! June 18th is Autistic Pride Day, which is about celebrating all things autistic! It is also about combating any feelings of shame that autistic people have been made to feel in the past about their identities. We shouldn't feel ashamed about who we are; we should be able to feel proud. That is why the concept of pride is so important to the autistic *and* to the LGBTQIA+ communities.

# ⇒ Chapter 3 ⇐

# Introducing Some Well-Known Autistic and Gender-Divergent People

There are many people who we can see as role models or examples within the autistic community and the transgender community – and some in both! This chapter features some well-known autistic people, gender divergent people and some well-known people who are both neurodivergent and gender divergent.

# WELL-KNOWN AUTISTIC PEOPLE

There are a number of well-known people who are autistic. These people have used their autistic traits, passions and interests to make the world a better place in their chosen areas of interest.

## Greta Thunberg

Greta Thunberg is a Swedish autistic teen and climate change activist. When Greta first learnt about climate change at the age of eight, she was shocked that adults didn't seem to be taking the crisis seriously. She became depressed. She didn't eat, go to school or speak for months. Her need to fight for the climate became her motivation. She made the decision never to fly, eat meat or dairy or buy unnecessary things.

But Greta saw that she needed to use her voice to do more. Greta founded the climate strike movement. Greta Thunberg's climate strikes mobilize people – particularly young people – to fight against climate change and pressure world leaders to take action on the climate crisis. Her parents had tried to stop her, but she was determined to see it through and sat down, alone. She wrote on Twitter: 'We children usually don't do as you tell us to do, we do as you do. And if you adults don't care about my future, neither do I.' The media took an immediate interest, and Greta's climate strike made the news. The movement has since become international. Greta has mobilized over seven million children across the world to strike, like her, for climate justice. Greta is one of the most influential people alive today, and she is autistic. Greta is living proof of the power of autistic people's passions and interests to change the world.

## Satoshi Tajiri

Satoshi Tajiri is the Japanese game designer who invented Pokémon. When he was a child, he loved collecting insects. Then, when he was a teenager, he really loved gaming. He had difficulties at school, but when he was in his late teens, he wrote and edited a gamer magazine called *Game Freak*, which had tips for gamers. That led Satoshi to realize that lots of games could be improved, so he designed one of his own, which incorporated his passion for bugs. Now people all over the world love Pokémon.

## Carly Fleischmann

Carly has a condition that results in her having problems getting speech messages from her brain to her mouth, so words don't come out. Carly uses a device in order to communicate. Many autistic people use devices in order to talk.

Carly is a media presenter. She uses text-to-voice technology to interview her guests. She types her questions onto her computer, which then reads them out. Her show is called 'Speechless', and she's very funny. Her very first guest was actor Channing Tatum.

Do you use any methods other than speech to communicate?

## The AutistiX

Several of the band members from the AutistiX are autistic! The AutistiX are a rock band from London, England. They met at a meet-up for musicians with disabilities and decided to form a band with a few other people.

The AutistiX use their music to help them express themselves socially in ways they find hard at other times. Their first music video was called 'Just the Same'. It is a song about inclusion and acceptance. It is available on YouTube, and it's definitely worth a listen. They really enjoy making music together. Often autistic people make friends with other autistic or neurodivergent people. Do you have any friends who are autistic or neurodivergent?

## Summer Farrelly

Summer is an autistic Australian teenager who invented a therapy programme called Chickens to Love, a therapy programme using chickens. It is for everyone who needs it – not just autistic people. The programme helps people to gain insight into emotions and social situations through bonding with chickens. Summer Farrelly also provides sensory materials for autistic children and young people. Summer loves chickens and, by carefully watching their behaviour, she noticed they have a complex social hierarchy. Summer thought the chickens acted a bit like people, because they have friendship groups and they don't all like each other, and they behave like people in other ways too.

Summer experiences hyper-empathy, which means that she feels other people's emotions. This is hard at times and is a very common experience for many autistic people. Watching the chickens has helped Summer learn about and understand how people act.

Summer's programme Chickens to Love lets other autistic kids take part too! Summer also does a lot of work with the autistic community and gives autistic kids sensory packs. She has done a lot of media interviews about her work and being autistic.

# WELL-KNOWN TRANSGENDER AND/OR NON-BINARY PEOPLE

There are many influential trans and gender-divergent people in the world, although the world could definitely benefit from more transgender people in public life. This is a list of some trans and gender-divergent people who are well known.

## Laverne Cox

Laverne Cox is a transgender actress who studied dance for many years before acting in TV shows such as *Law & Order* and the reality show *TRANSform Me*. Her breakthrough role was as role of

Sophia Burset in the popular Netflix series *Orange Is the New Black*. This made her the first trans woman of colour to have a leading role on a mainstream television drama series. She became the first openly transgender person in history to be nominated for an Emmy Award. Cox is a passionate advocate for trans and LGBTQIA+ rights. Laverne also has her own podcast.

## Georgina Beyer

Can trans people be politicians and public officials? Yes! Georgina Beyer is a transgender politician in New Zealand. In the 1980s, she affirmed her gender as a trans woman and became a singer and drag performer in a Wellington nightclub. After that, she got a chance to become the local news presenter as a radio host in Wairarapa.

Georgina became mayor of the small town of Carterton, New Zealand, in 1995, making her the first transgender mayor in New Zealand. She was then selected as the Labour Party's candidate for the 1999 election. She became the first transgender member of parliament in the world. In addition. She was also re-elected for the Labour Party in the 2002 and 2005 New Zealand elections.

# Sam Smith

Sam Smith is a well-known recording artist who came out as non-binary in 2019. You might have heard some of Sam's songs like 'Too Good at Goodbyes', 'Fire on Fire' or 'Dancing with a Stranger'. Sam's pronouns are they/them. Smith said on their coming out: 'After a lifetime of being at war with my gender I've decided to embrace myself for who I am, inside and out.' Sam also said: 'I'm not male or female, I think I flow somewhere in between. It's all on the spectrum.' Smith described being non-binary as 'your own special creation'.

Sam said that they want to be 'visible and open' about their gender identity.

It is wonderful to have celebrities who are out as non-binary and transgender, as it can make it easier for us to be proud of who we are, if that is what we want. Sam Smith being out makes it easier for other trans and non-binary people to be out, even if we are not famous!

# Elliot Page

Elliot Page is a Canadian actor and producer who has starred in many films including *Juno*, *Inception* and quirky comedy *Whip It*. Elliot was a child star and had won awards for his acting by the time he was

18. Elliot came out as a trans man in December 2020. Elliot posted this statement to his social media:

Hi friends, I want to share with you that I am trans, my pronouns are he/they and my name is Elliot. I feel lucky to be writing this. To be here. To have arrived at this place in my life... I can't begin to express how remarkable it feels to finally love who I am enough to pursue my authentic self. I've been endlessly inspired by so many in the trans community. Thank you for your courage, your generosity and ceaselessly working to make this world a more inclusive and compassionate place. I will offer whatever support I can and continue to strive for a more loving and equal society.

Elliot is an example of a trans person who has a lot of influence in popular culture and is making a difference for all of us through being out loud and proud.

# WELL-KNOWN AUTISTIC AND GENDER-DIVERGENT PEOPLE

## Hannah Gadsby

Hannah Gadsby is an Australian comedian best known for her shows *Nanette* (2017) and *Douglas*

(2019). Hannah was diagnosed with ADHD and autism in 2017. She referred to her autism in her show *Douglas* in a way that was aimed to help people understand neurodiversity and neurodivergent experiences. Hannah identifies as gender non-conforming and lesbian and is a very public supporter – and example – of queer pride. Hannah went to art school and has a keen interest in visual art and in particular an interest in challenging the patriarchy in visual art. Hannah Gadsby can be seen as a great role model for the autistic and queer communities.

## Dr Wenn B. Lawson

Dr Wenn B. Lawson is an autistic and trans author, academic and advocate. Wenn has been writing about autism since the 1990s. Wenn came out as trans relatively recently. He has written a number of papers and books about the transgender experience for autistic people, including the memoir he wrote with his wife Beatrice, *Transitioning Together* (JKP, 2017), and *The Autistic Trans Guide to Life* (JKP, 2021), co-authored with Yenn Purkis – one of the authors of this book! Wenn has contributed a lot of knowledge around autism and especially gender diversity and autism.

# Laura Kate Dale

Laura Kate Dale is an autistic and transgender lesbian and the author of the book *Uncomfortable Labels* (JKP, 2019). Laura's book is an autobiography focussing on her life growing up autistic, trans and gay. The book has sold a lot of copies and is a great addition to writing about autism, sexuality and gender diversity.

## ACTIVITY: Do you know anyone else who could be included in the list in this chapter?

1. . . . . . . . . . . . . . . . . . . . . . . . . . . . . . . . . . . . . . . . . .

2. . . . . . . . . . . . . . . . . . . . . . . . . . . . . . . . . . . . . . . . . .

3. . . . . . . . . . . . . . . . . . . . . . . . . . . . . . . . . . . . . . . . . .

We hope you have enjoyed this chapter and that it gives you a sense of the great people in the neurodivergent and gender-divergent communities and those whose experience intersects both. We really do have some amazing role models.

# ⇒ Chapter 4 ⇐

# Being Trans and Autistic

# ALL ABOUT PUBERTY — EXPERIENCES OF TRANS KIDS AND TEENS

Going through puberty for anyone can be pretty strange and scary: our bodies, voices, and faces start to change, and we notice that people begin treating us differently, we are given more responsibilities and we are expected to act in more grown-up ways. Puberty also brings on a lot of emotional changes: emotions might start to get 'louder' in your body; for example, you might feel embarrassment much more strongly than before, or you might find you get annoyed or upset more easily than before.

Everyone will experience puberty differently and will have a different combination of changes. Some of these changes are associated with a particular gender identity — e.g. experiencing periods is associated with being a cis girl — but this is not true in the world of gender diversity! Non-binary, intersex and trans-boys can experience periods too. For this reason, we have listed changes without labelling them with a gender or particular kind of biology.

Here is a list of some of the changes that might happen:

- Voice changes

- Skin becomes oilier, pimples begin to appear

- New hair growth on face, underarms, torso and genitals

- Height and weight changes, stretch marks appear

- Body shape changes, e.g. shoulders and hips can get wider

- Breasts develop

- Experiencing periods

- Experiencing erections

- Changes in appetite, feeling hungrier than usual

- Needing more sleep, being more tired

- Changes in emotions, feeling 'moody', self-conscious, sad or angry

- Changes in meltdowns or shutdowns

- Experiencing sexual or romantic attraction.

For autistic and trans kids, puberty can be an extra troubling time. There might be a lot of changes that happen quickly that you don't feel prepared for. Puberty can make gender dysphoria louder in trans and gender-divergent kids because it might bring out characteristics that you don't associate with your gender identity. It is important to reach out to someone you trust if you are struggling with the effects of puberty.

# HORMONES

Hormones influence how we think, feel and look. Our hormone levels change a lot with puberty, and this is what leads to the physical and emotional changes listed above.

Hormones have all different kinds of roles in our bodies, including some that influence how 'feminine' or 'masculine' our bodies look. These hormones are called *oestrogen* and *testosterone*. Although oestrogen is thought of as a *feminizing* hormone, and testosterone is thought of as a *masculinizing* hormone, everyone has a combination of both testosterone and oestrogen in their bodies, regardless of their gender identity. These hormones work together to influence how your body changes with puberty.

Some trans and gender-divergent people will want to change their hormone levels in order to better reflect their gender identity to themselves and the world. To do this, they can undergo a form of therapy called hormone replacement therapy, or HRT for short. HRT helps to change the levels of testosterone or oestrogen you have in your body in order to change your appearance to be more masculine or more feminine. Lots of people have strong opinions about HRT, and you might too. This can feel very confusing and overwhelming, and you might worry about whether you want to try HRT or not. There is nothing wrong with wanting HRT. Even if you feel pressured not to by friends or family, there are people who you can talk to.

Seeking HRT is a long process that involves accessing and speaking to multiple medical professionals. There are guidelines around the minimum age someone might receive HRT, which is different across countries and regions. Generally, it is around age 16 in the US, UK and Australia when medical professionals will trust you to make an informed decision about starting HRT, but this will vary depending on your own unique circumstances. If you decide you do want HRT, there is a chance you will need to wait until you are older to access it. An option for the meantime can be to take 'puberty blockers', which temporarily block the effects of puberty and can be useful if you want more time to make a decision. The minimum age around puberty blockers isn't set; it will depend on your own circumstances again. It is important to seek professional support so they can speak to you about how you can access these things. We have listed some reputable organizations to seek information from at the end of this book.

Not all trans and gender-divergent people will want to seek HRT, and that is OK! You don't have to take HRT to be trans or gender divergent; you do not need to prove your gender identity to others by doing anything that you are unsure of or do not want to. HRT is just one form of gender affirmation. Others might find that socially transitioning (e.g. changing their gender-identity label, clothing style, hair style, name or pronouns), is what is needed to help them feel 'at home' in themself. Whatever you decide is OK; it's your body and your life.

It is important you and your parents do your own research, listen to the experiences of others who are on a similar path and speak with a professional who specializes in working with trans and gender-divergent young people. There is heaps of information available online, but you should look at information that comes from recommended organizations and experts, especially those that are led by trans and gender-divergent people themselves! There are many non-experts who will share false and harmful information online, who will try to trick you into feeling bad about your identity. Don't listen to them. If you think something you are reading or watching is mean or hurtful, it is a good idea to talk to someone you trust who understands what you are going through.

Remember, if you are interested in any therapy, especially HRT, even if you are just curious to ask some questions and hear more, it is important to talk to your doctor and visit a gender clinic or a psychologist who specializes in youth transgender health.

# TALKING TO MEDICAL PROFESSIONALS

Medical professionals include doctors, psychologists, psychiatrists, therapists, speech pathologists and occupational therapists. If you are experiencing gender dysphoria, thinking about medical interventions like hormones or surgeries, having a hard time with your mental health or just want someone to talk to, it is best to speak with an experienced medical professional for support.

A good place to start can be asking for help from trusted grown-ups, like parents, your school counsellor, a doctor or a youth mental health service. Once you speak to them, they can often refer you on to someone with more specialist expertise. If you get nervous talking to grown-ups about this stuff, you can write some notes on what you want to say and bring them with you on the day. You could even just hand them the notes if you don't want to say some things out loud.

Unfortunately, some medical practitioners can be transphobic, or they might not understand your needs properly. This isn't OK. You deserve support and understanding. If you feel like the person you have gone to isn't being supportive or is being transphobic, you do not have to continue to see them. You can try speaking with someone else and can also make a complaint. You should be able to find someone supportive where you feel listened to and understood.

## CHANGING YOUR NAME

Some people will want to change their name to something that fits better. This will involve thinking about lots of different names, trying some of them out and deciding which names feel best!

Some tips for 'trying on' different names can be:

- Asking certain people to call you a particular name so you can see how it feels to hear it from others

- Going to a cafe where they take a name alongside your order, so you can hear a stranger call it out

- Writing it down and seeing how it looks

- Practising writing new signatures

- Using it in your online spaces such as in games, in forums or on social media.

Like clothes, you won't know what fits until you try it on. There is no rush to decide on a name. It is an important part of your identity, so you will want to think about it. It is OK to take your time, and it is OK to have some fun trying out different choices before making any big decisions.

You might not want to legally change your name; you could choose nicknames or abbreviations of your name that you think suit you. For example, Sam's full name is 'Samson', and they get to choose whether they want to be called 'Sam' or 'Samson'. They could even just call themselves 'S' if they wanted!

# ALL ABOUT TOILETS

Public toilets are gendered spaces, which means that they are often labelled as 'men's' and 'women's'. This can be really uncomfortable if you are questioning your gender identity or if you aren't sure how your gender will be perceived by others. Most places will have an accessible toilet and sometimes this will also be called a gender-neutral toilet, and this may be the safest option for you to use. Some places will have all gender-neutral toilets, which can be a great relief! It can be useful to note what kinds of toilets are available in the places you visit. For example, at school, there might be some gender-neutral toilets or toilets that are in a more private location that you can use more comfortably. You can talk to your school about what you would prefer, whether it is using a different toilet than what you used to, the same toilets or the accessible toilet.

The main thing to remember about toilets is not to let them define you. Just because you use the women's toilets doesn't make you a woman and using the men's toilets doesn't make you a man. Your gender identity is yours, and how you choose to act in response to your gender identity is up to you. If you are feeling nervous, you could always get a friend, trusted grown-up or teacher to wait outside for you.

It might be best to have a conversation with your trusted grown-ups, school or workplace to talk about what they can do to support you to access the toilet you feel most comfortable with.

# ALL ABOUT PRONOUNS

Pronouns are words that identify us – they are kind of like a secondary name. You can choose which pronouns suit you; you can choose one set of pronouns or many. It is up to you. There are many pronouns to choose from, including some less-known pronouns called neo-pronouns, which offer some alternatives to he or she. People might express confusion around using neo-pronouns, but they are here to stay!

Some pronouns:

- She/her/hers

- He/him/his

- They/them/theirs

- Xe/xem/xeirs (pronounced *zee/zem/zeers*)

- Thon/thon/thons

- Your name!

- Nounself pronouns: Choose any word you like and that can be your pronoun (e.g. flower/flowerself/flowers, frog/frogself/frogs). This can be really tricky for people to learn and understand at first, but once you've practised a few times, it can start to feel more natural to say. It is a good idea to practise using uncommon pronouns in sentences with family or friends you are close to!

Sharing and using pronouns can be an important way to express gender identity. It can be great to practise using different pronouns to try them out and see how you feel hearing them. You could ask close friends and family to help you to trial pronouns to see how you feel when you hear them being spoken or written about you.

Remember, using your pronouns is a basic sign of respect. While it might be difficult to get the hang of at first, it is important that people in your life make the effort to use your pronouns.

# ACTIVITY: Practise writing a different name or pronouns

Here is some space to practise writing down different pronouns in sentences. You could write sentences describing yourself or someone else's interests and characteristics. You could even read them aloud to practise hearing them spoken. This could also be an activity that you do with a friend or family member so that you get to practise and learn together.

Here are some examples:

- He/him: '*He* is great at drawing; I can't wait to see *him* share *his* latest picture.'

- They/them: 'I like *their* hat; it really suits *them*.'

- Xe/xem: 'I met Alex the other day; *xe* were really nice and I want to spend time with *xem* again.'

- Frog/frogself: 'I bought *frog* a new book today; *frog* likes to read fantasy books. *Frog* said *frog* will lend me *frog's* book when *frog* has finished it.'

. . . . . . . . . . . . . . . . . . . . . . . . . . . . . . . . . . . . . . . . . . .

. . . . . . . . . . . . . . . . . . . . . . . . . . . . . . . . . . . . . . . . . . .

. . . . . . . . . . . . . . . . . . . . . . . . . . . . . . . . . . . . . . . . . . .

. . . . . . . . . . . . . . . . . . . . . . . . . . . . . . . . . . . . . . . . . . .

. . . . . . . . . . . . . . . . . . . . . . . . . . . . . . . . . . . . . . . . . . .

. . . . . . . . . . . . . . . . . . . . . . . . . . . . . . . . . . . . . . . . . . .

. . . . . . . . . . . . . . . . . . . . . . . . . . . . . . . . . . . . . . . . . . .

. . . . . . . . . . . . . . . . . . . . . . . . . . . . . . . . . . . . . . . . . . .

. . . . . . . . . . . . . . . . . . . . . . . . . . . . . . . . . . . . . . . . . . .

. . . . . . . . . . . . . . . . . . . . . . . . . . . . . . . . . . . . . . . . . . .

# ⇌ Chapter 5 ⇋

# All About Coming Out

# WHAT IS COMING OUT AND WHY IS IT IMPORTANT?

Coming out means telling others in your life about your gender identity and/or sexuality. People you might come out to include your family members, friends, teachers, employer (if you have one) or health professionals.

Coming out usually involves having a conversation with someone and saying you are trans/gender divergent. You may need to come out to many different people on different occasions. It can be quite stressful to come out, especially to family members. Coming out conversations benefit from some preparation. You can think about what you want to say, who you want to say it to, how much you want to say and what you want from the person you are coming out to.

Coming out is a very important element of being trans and gender divergent. It is where we tell those we care about and spend time with about a very important part of what makes us who we are: our gender identity. While it can be a difficult thing to do, coming out is a great opportunity to be positive about who we are and share our gender-diversity journey with those in our life.

# COMING OUT CONVERSATION GUIDE

This template can be used to help plan your coming out conversation. Feel free to add your own experiences and change it — it is just a guide to help prepare you for having a coming out conversation.

Hi,

*I want to talk to you about something.*

*I have known this for some time but I haven't told you yet. I have been thinking about my gender and I now know that I am [insert: transgender, a girl, a boy, non-binary, or other]. I am telling you because I want you to know this about me and understand where I am coming from. This means that [insert what it means for you]. This is very important to me. My gender identity is a key part of who I am. I would like to be known by the pronouns [insert: he, she, they, xe, other]. I would like to change my name to [insert]. What I need from you is support, understanding and respect. I am learning about my identity too and don't know everything about my gender. Thank you for understanding. I will try to answer any questions you have but I may not be able to.*

# WHAT DO YOU DO IF IT GOES BADLY?

Sometimes the coming out conversation will go badly. This is not your fault and is usually the result of the person you are coming out to being transphobic or struggling to understand. Even so, it can be very upsetting and stressful when this happens. Be aware that people's attitudes and prejudices can change. Even if the person responds badly the first time you talk about your gender, they may change their thinking in the future. If someone is hostile to you for being trans, then it is their issue, not yours. It may be wise to distance yourself from that person as it may not be safe – physically or emotionally – to be around them.

It can be difficult if close family members react badly to your coming out. Sometimes transgender young people have to move out of their home or have no contact with family. This is very sad, and it is never OK to discriminate against trans people this way. It is also never the fault of the transgender young person. We hope this doesn't ever happen to you. Many trans people create a 'family of choice'. This is a group of people who they are close to and who perform the function of a family if biological family members reject them due to bigotry and transphobia. Families of choice are often trans and gender divergent people themselves and those who *get it*.

# DO YOU NEED TO COME OUT?

You do not need to come out if you do not want to. However, if you are considering medical interventions around your gender such as surgery or hormones or if you change how you express your gender (such as through wearing different clothes or a binder) or change your name, then it is a good idea to have a conversation about your gender with those who are close to you. Most transgender people come out to at least some of the people in their lives. You have every right to come out and be and express to others who you truly are. While coming out can be difficult, many trans and gender-divergent people come out and are happy to do so. Living in the closet has its own difficulties. The decision to come out is your own. It may take a while for you to build up the courage and resolve to come out, and that is OK. Alternatively, you may want to come out as soon as you realize you are transgender. That is OK as well. There is no right or wrong approach when it comes to coming out.

# TALKING ABOUT YOUR GENDER

It is likely that you will want to talk about your gender to people in your life. This can be quite challenging, especially if the people you talk to are not supportive. Many autistic people find talking to other people – especially non-autistic people – difficult anyway, so adding something as personal as your gender identity into the conversation can be difficult.

Here are some tips for talking about your gender with different people in your life.

# Friends

You may have friends who are autistic, and you may have friends who are also gender divergent. These friends are likely to be easier to talk to than non-autistic and/or cisgender friends. Fellow autistic people often *get* other autistic people, so the conversation about gender may be as simple as just saying, 'I am transgender' and explaining what that may mean.

With neurotypical friends and cisgender friends, you might need to share a little more about your gender, such as what it feels like to be trans or what you will do to transition gender (such as changing your name and pronouns or taking hormones). You do not need to have all the answers, and it is OK to say that your transition is something that will develop over time.

# Parents

Talking to your parents about your gender is something many people find extremely challenging. Of course, it depends on your parents' attitudes around gender diversity and the relationship you have with them. Hopefully they will be respectful and supportive, but this isn't always the case.

It can help to schedule a time with your parents and tell them beforehand that you have something you need to discuss. When you speak with your parents, you can tell them about your gender – what it means for you, how it is something you have been thinking about for some time, how you need them to support you and respect your decision to transition.

If your parents respond badly, there are a few things you can do. One is to remind yourself that sometimes parents need some time to come to terms with things. Your transition may be a very big deal for your parents too – although probably for different reasons to you. Your parents may need a while to come to terms with your identity. While it is very upsetting when parents respond badly, this does not necessarily have to be a permanent response. There are support services for gender-diverse kids such as Minus 18 in Australia, Mermaids in the UK and Trans Youth Equality Foundation in

North America. These services are there to support you in just this kind of situation.

## Siblings

Having a conversation about your gender with siblings can also be challenging, depending on your relationship with them. If you have younger siblings, your coming out can be a lovely thing and make you a trans role model for your younger sibs. Sometimes relationships with older siblings can be difficult, so you might want to plan your coming out conversation similarly to how you do the conversation with your parents. If siblings do not immediately support you, it is possible their attitudes may change over time.

## New people

Often transgender people are assumed – incorrectly – to be a different gender to the one they affirm. This often happens when we meet someone new and they make assumptions. Being misgendered as 'she' when you are trans male or non-binary is often very upsetting. When we meet new people, it is common to be misgendered and it can be hard to know what to say in response.

It can be difficult to call someone out on misgendering us. Sometimes an ally, such as a friend or parent, can speak on our behalf and correct the misgendering. Sometimes we can stand up for ourselves and explain that we are not a 'she' (or a 'he'). Trans people shouldn't have to be responsible for educating everyone in the world about gender diversity, but sometimes we – or our allies – do need to correct someone getting it wrong. Calling someone out on getting our pronouns, gender or name wrong also helps other trans people by making them aware of gender diversity.

## ACTIVITY: What are some things you would like people in your life (family, friends, etc.) to know about you?

. . . . . . . . . . . . . . . . . . . . . . . . . . . . . . . . . . . . . . . . . . .

. . . . . . . . . . . . . . . . . . . . . . . . . . . . . . . . . . . . . . . . . . .

. . . . . . . . . . . . . . . . . . . . . . . . . . . . . . . . . . . . . . . . . . .

. . . . . . . . . . . . . . . . . . . . . . . . . . . . . . . . . . . . . . . . . . .

· · · · · · · · · · · · · · · · · · · · · · · · · · · · · · · · · · · · · · · · · · · · · · · · ·

· · · · · · · · · · · · · · · · · · · · · · · · · · · · · · · · · · · · · · · · · · · · · · · · ·

· · · · · · · · · · · · · · · · · · · · · · · · · · · · · · · · · · · · · · · · · · · · · · · · ·

· · · · · · · · · · · · · · · · · · · · · · · · · · · · · · · · · · · · · · · · · · · · · · · · ·

· · · · · · · · · · · · · · · · · · · · · · · · · · · · · · · · · · · · · · · · · · · · · · · · ·

· · · · · · · · · · · · · · · · · · · · · · · · · · · · · · · · · · · · · · · · · · · · · · · · ·

# ⋟ Chapter 6 ⋞

# Challenges of Being Trans and Autistic

# WHY BEING TRANS AND AUTISTIC CAN SOMETIMES BE HARD

Being trans or gender divergent and autistic is a fairly unique experience, so your perspective on the world might be different to peers or family members. While it is good to have your own perspectives, this can also mean that it is hard to find ways to share how you see things with others. You might feel like no one else will understand you. But don't worry, there are plenty of other teens working through the same challenges that you are.

Everybody in the world experiences all different kinds of challenges and has to come up with ways to overcome them. Some challenges are better known than others. Being unique comes with unique challenges, so these might be a bit less known, but they are still just as important. In this chapter we will talk about what some of these challenges are and some strategies to work through them.

We might feel misunderstood, and we may even be discriminated against for being different, and this is not OK. Everyone deserves to be treated with respect regardless of their gender identity or the way their brain is wired. It is important to be able to express yourself authentically, without being worried about being judged or treated badly as a result.

# WHAT IS TRANSPHOBIA AND WHY IT IS NOT OK

Transphobia refers to discrimination based on being transgender. It could be people calling you mean names, intentionally using incorrect pronouns to refer to you, insulting your gender identity or not letting you use gendered spaces, such as toilets or sports teams, that align with your gender identity. Transphobia comes in all shapes and sizes; it can be really obvious or it can be subtle. Sometimes, it might be hard to tell whether something is transphobic or not. If it makes you uncomfortable, it's OK to listen to that feeling and to say something, even if you just say, 'What you just said makes me feel uneasy.' It lets the person you are with know where your boundaries are when talking about gender stuff. You can always tell that person in the future if you figure out what exactly it was that made you uncomfortable, or if it no longer makes you feel uneasy.

Sometimes people can say or do things that are transphobic because they are ignorant, and they just don't know any better yet. Other times, people can be transphobic because they want to cause hurt towards other people. Regardless of whether someone *intends* to be transphobic or not, transphobia still hurts the same, and is still unacceptable. If you feel brave enough, then call it out. Just because transphobia exists in our world doesn't mean it's OK.

We all need to feel a sense of belonging in our community, and we need to feel like we can express ourselves the way we want without being discriminated against. These are basic needs that everyone has. Meeting these needs might be more difficult because others might not want to express themselves the way you do, or they might be afraid that people will be mean. You might like to experiment with pronouns or with your clothing style and find friends who do this too. This is a great way to connect with others, but sometimes it can be tricky finding others who you live close to who also want to explore their gender.

Experiencing transphobia can be very upsetting. It can be helpful to talk to a trusted counsellor or psychologist who understands gender diversity to work on strategies to advocate for yourself, manage anxiety and practise self-care. It can be difficult to find support services that can actually support you as an autistic person *and* as a trans or gender-divergent person. This is especially difficult if you live in a place that isn't LGBTQIA+ friendly. The trick is not to give up and to keep searching for support that feels right to you.

The transgender community has a long and proud history; we have fought for our right to express ourselves and be heard and supported just like anyone else. It is important that the transgender community stands together and supports each other to express ourselves in the way that we feel most comfortable. Whether we are gender non-conforming, non-binary, queer or binary transgender, we all deserve the right to express ourselves.

# GENDER DYSPHORIA

Gender dysphoria can come from feeling like parts of your body don't fit with your gender identity. There are many expectations placed on bodies in our society, and it is important to remember that just because others have these expectations doesn't mean that you have to. You deserve to feel comfortable in your own body and to make your own choices about it. It can be really difficult to manage gender dysphoria because it can feel like we are bombarded non-stop with gendered language and expectations about what you 'should' look like. These ideas can conflict with your own sense of gender and lead you to feel disconnected from your body. You might feel like your body isn't 'yours' or that it doesn't match how you feel on the inside. It is important to speak to someone you trust if you feel this way. There are many options for treatment to try out.

Gender dysphoria is very real and can be debilitating. Left untreated, gender dysphoria can lead to things like anxiety or depression, so it is really important that you seek help if you are experiencing discomfort around your gender identity.

Like gender identity, bodies come in all shapes and sizes. There is no such thing as a 'man's body' or a 'woman's body'. You might wish that your body looked more masculine or more feminine to represent how you feel on the inside; this is your gender expression, which basically means how you choose to express your internal sense of your gender.

## WHAT DO YOU DO IF SOMEONE BULLIES YOU?

Bullying can be extremely hurtful and difficult to deal with. It is OK to feel angry or upset if you are getting bullied. Bullying is never OK.

If you are experiencing bullying at school, online or anywhere else, it is really important that you speak to someone who can support you. This should be an adult who you trust like a teacher, counsellor or family member. People bully others to make themselves feel better or to distract attention away from themselves. Although sometimes people are bullies because they have experienced bullying themselves, this still does not make it OK.

## ACTIVITY: List five different people or organizations that you can reach out to if you are struggling with transphobia or bullying

1. . . . . . . . . . . . . . . . . . . . . . . . . . . . . . . . . . . . . . . . . . . . .

2. . . . . . . . . . . . . . . . . . . . . . . . . . . . . . . . . . . . . . . . . . . . .

3. . . . . . . . . . . . . . . . . . . . . . . . . . . . . . . . . . . . . . . . . . . . .

4. . . . . . . . . . . . . . . . . . . . . . . . . . . . . . . . . . . . . . . . . . . . .

5. . . . . . . . . . . . . . . . . . . . . . . . . . . . . . . . . . . . . . . . . . . . .

## RESPONDING TO DIFFICULT COMMENTS

You might get lots of questions or comments from people about your identity. This can be overwhelming and exhausting at times, especially if you find yourself saying the same things over and over again. If this happens, it is a good idea to take some time to find ways to make it easier for you to respond. It is OK to take your time in responding, even to go away and have some thinking time before responding to what someone has said.

Sometimes, a comment that someone says can make you feel uncomfortable but you might not know exactly why. In this situation, it might be a good idea to chat to someone who does understand you. They might be able to help you unpack this feeling and come up with a response that you can give the person.

If you do want to learn about ways to talk about gender identity safely with others, you might find resources at your local mental health services, at local youth services, at a gender clinic or online. For example, minus18.org.au is an Australian website that offers resources for talking about gender identity with others.

There are some very common questions and comments that we hear from other people regarding gender identity. Below, we have come up with some suggested responses for you to use to these common statements. You are welcome to practise writing your own versions of responses down too:

- 'But you aren't *really*...(a girl/a boy/non-binary/ etc.)'

    o 'I am . . . . . . . . . . . . . . . This is how I feel on the inside, and this is how I describe myself. It is how I understand myself. It is important to me that you respect what I am telling you.'

- ■ 'Autistic people don't really understand their gender identity...'

  - O 'Many autistic people feel similarly to me. I feel strongly about my gender identity, and I am comfortable in my understanding. I want your support and acceptance to help me feel safer expressing myself.'

- ■ 'Why do you have to put labels on things? Can't you just be you?'

  - O 'We are given labels by other people all of the time. I want to be able to choose my own labels rather than have people put labels on me that I disagree with. The labels I choose are important to me, and it means a lot to me to have them respected.'

- ■ 'What if you change your mind?'

  - O 'This is how I understand myself right now. My understanding of myself will grow, and maybe I will find new labels or names or pronouns to better express who I am, but this is how you can support me at the moment...e.g. by referring to me with . . . . . . . . . . . pronouns, and by calling me . . . . . . . . . . instead of . . . . . . . . . . . .'

- 'It's just too hard. I can't keep up with all these pronouns and labels. I don't know what to say.'

  - o 'It doesn't have to be hard. If you don't know what to say, you can always ask me. I can share some resources with you (including this book!) that might help you learn. It really shows that you care when you use correct pronouns and labels. They might be new to you, but they are here to stay.'

- 'I don't want you to change your body.'

  - o 'I am not doing this for anyone else but myself. The decisions I make around my own body are mine. It is about me growing up into who I want to be.'

- 'There are only two genders...'

  - o 'If you want to limit gender diversity to two boxes, that is your decision. I do not see gender like that. I am comfortable with my understanding of gender diversity, and my viewpoint is not up for discussion with you.'

- If someone uses part of your identity as a slur, e.g. 'That's so autistic.'

  o 'That's a really mean way to use that term. I don't want to hear you using that term as an insult. There is nothing wrong with being autistic.'

Some other responses you can use:

- 'I don't want to talk to someone who is being disrespectful.'

- 'Please don't say hurtful things when you obviously don't understand what you are talking about.'

Finally, remember that you do not owe anyone an explanation for who you are. You know yourself best, and no one else gets to decide who you are. You do not need to justify yourself to anyone else, and you do not need to answer questions that people ask if you do not want to.

## Chapter 7

# Ways to Make Life Easier

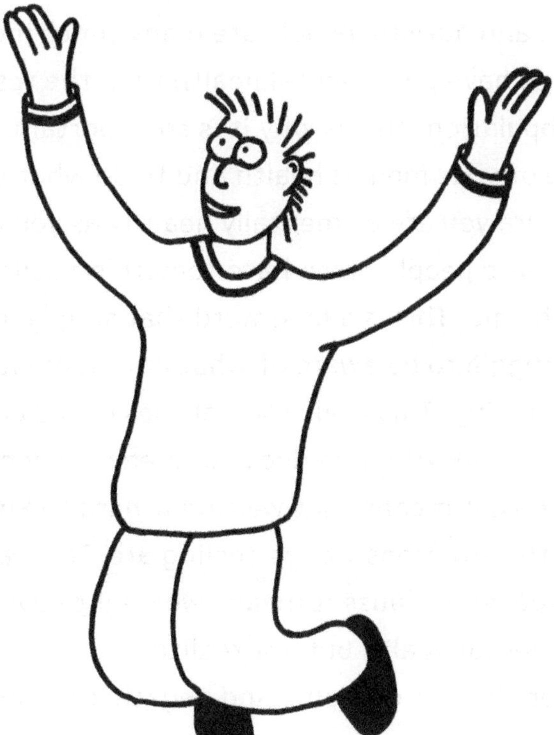

# MANAGING YOUR MENTAL HEALTH

Mental health is very important for everyone. It is especially important for trans and gender-divergent people, for autistic people and for young people.

Mental health is one of the most important things we have. If you have good mental health, it makes life that much easier. If you have poor mental health, it can affect every part of your life and make it difficult. Trans and gender-divergent people and autistic people are many times more likely to have poor mental health than the rest of the population. This is why it is so important to be aware of your mental health and to do what you can to ensure you are as mentally healthy as you can be.

Autistic people often have something called alexithymia. This is a long word that simply means we struggle to be aware of what emotions we are experiencing. This is also sometimes called emotion blindness. Alexithymia does not mean we don't have emotions. It means that we find it hard to know what the emotions we are feeling are. This can be a big problem because it means we might have very poor mental health but not realize it.

There is a lot of blame and negativity around mental health, sometimes known as stigma. Stigma means that some people are prejudiced about mental health. This means that many people do not want to talk about their mental health and think it is shameful. Mental illness is actually very common, and stigma is really unhelpful. There is nothing shameful about having poor mental health. Would you judge someone who had heart disease or who broke their leg? Of course you wouldn't! In a similar way, mental illness is nothing to be ashamed of, and a person with mental illness has as much right to respect and helpful treatment as a person with heart disease or a broken leg would.

Some things can make your mental health worse, and some can make it better. These are often called risk factors and protective factors. Risk factors can make your mental health worse and protective factors can make it better.

Risk factors related to mental health include things like:

- High levels of stress

- People being hateful towards you

- Bullying

- Transphobia/homophobia/etc.

- Discrimination because you are autistic or neurodivergent

- People telling you that you are incapable or other negative messages

- Trolling

- Failure/mistakes

- Abuse and violence

- Trauma, including things that make you fear for your life or safety

- Low self-confidence or self-esteem

- A mental illness such as depression, anxiety, bipolar disorder, post-traumatic stress, schizophrenia and others.

There are some things you can do to help improve your mental health. These include:

- Seeing a mental health professional like a psychologist or psychiatrist if you are having a hard time. In some countries you can access mental health support for free.

- Learning to like and value yourself. This is great for good mental health.

- Practising some strategies, like distraction. Distraction is exactly what it sounds like – focussing on something other than whatever your brain is doing. Each person has different distractions that work for them. Distractions can include gaming, reading, listening to music, watching TV, talking with friends and many other things. Find a distraction that works for you.

- Engaging in your passionate interests. One of the best things about being autistic is our passionate interests. This can be a great mental health strategy.

- Spending time with pets and assistance animals. A great many autistic people, although not all of us, respond really well to animals. Animals can be great mental health supports.

- Ending toxic friendships and relationships. It can be hard to know when a relationship or friendship is toxic. A good way to approach this is to reflect on how you feel when with a person. If you feel anxious and trapped, then the relationship may be toxic. If you are scared when around the person and the main elements of the relationship are conflict and argument, then the person may be toxic. We always think it is better not to have any relationship than to have a toxic one.

- Spending time with your neurodivergent and/ or trans friends.

- Some people benefit from medication for mental health issues and for ADHD/ADD. Medications work differently for each person, and it can take a few tries before you find the one that works best for you. Medications are usually prescribed by a psychiatrist or general practitioner.

- Taking a break from social media if it is causing you stress. Social media can be a great place to connect and share thoughts and experiences. However, it can also be bad for our mental health and wellbeing when there is trolling and hatred, which is sadly all too common. If your anxiety spikes every time you go online or see a response to your posts, it might be helpful to take a break for a while.

# THE IMPORTANCE OF FAMILY — THE ONE YOU ARE BORN WITH AND/OR THE ONE YOU CHOOSE

Everyone needs people in their life that love and care for them. For many people, this is the family they are born into. However, a person's birth family may not always be kind, supportive or helpful. For some trans and gender-divergent people, their birth family is not a safe place. Some family members can be hateful and transphobic. They can be the last people we want to spend time with. This is really sad, and it is the hateful family members who are at fault, not the trans person.

Society — especially media and popular culture — often dictates that we need to be close to members of our biological family. Family is viewed as a safe and loving place. Sadly, for many of us this is simply not true. For some people, being around their biological family is actually unsafe. Even so, people need a group of fellow humans who like, respect and care for them.  This means that many trans and gender-divergent people need to create a family of choice — a family that loves and respects them. If you need to make a family of choice, then look for people you like and who like you. Your close friends can form your family of choice, as can supportive members of your biological family.

You do not need to have been discriminated against by your biological family to have a family of choice. Many people simply add people to their family who are loving and supportive, even if their biological family is supportive as well. There are not really any rules around this. Simply try to surround yourself with people who love and care for you. For autistic people, this often includes other autistic and neurodivergent people, but there is no rule that says it has to.

## ACTIVITY: Can you think of some ways in which you can improve your mental health and wellbeing?

1. ....................................................

2. ....................................................

3. ....................................................

## WHERE DO YOU GO FOR SUPPORT?

Life can be challenging for trans and gender-divergent young people and teens. Often we need to find people or groups that support and care for us. Where do we do this?

There are many resources out there for gender-divergent and autistic people.

## Books

There are a number of books for autistic and trans and gender-divergent people. These include:

- *Uncomfortable Labels* by Laura Kate Dale (JKP, 2019). This is an autobiographical book looking at the author's life as a transgender autistic lesbian.

- *The Autistic Trans Guide to Life* by Wenn Lawson and Yenn Purkis (JKP, 2021). This is similar to this book but aimed at adults. There is a lot of information in the book that is relevant to teens as well.

- *Coming Out, Again* by Sabrina Symington (JKP, 2021). This is a graphic novel following a number of trans and neurodivergent characters.

- *Trans Teen Survival Guide* by Owl Fisher and Fox Fisher. This is a survival guide for trans teens. It isn't exclusively for autistic teens, but there are some really useful tips and strategies for trans teens.

## Websites

- Minus 18 – support for LGBTQIA+ young people: www.minus18.org.au

- Spectrum Intersections – gender diversity and autism support and advocacy: www. spectrumintersections.org

- A Gender Agenda – support and information for trans and gender-divergent people: https://genderrights.org.au

- LGBTQIA+ advocacy organization GLAAD has some transgender resources: www.glaad.org/ transgender/resources

- The Trevor Project – support for trans and gender-divergent young people: www. thetrevorproject.org

There are a number of online groups across different platforms where trans and gender-divergent and autistic young people can go for support and to connect with peers. If you would like to connect with these groups, we suggest contacting youth, gender-diversity and/or mental health organizations in your area and asking for recommendations or, alternatively, asking your trans and gender-divergent and/or autistic friends for recommendations of groups that they have found helpful.

## ALL THE BEST...

And so, this is it. You have come to the end of the book!

We hope you found it really helpful and that you understand more about autism, gender diversity and yourself – and know that you are an amazing person. There are many amazing autistic and trans people out there – and you just might be one of them! So, all the best from Sam and Yenn. Go forth and be wonderful and be proud of who you are.

# Glossary

**Agender** – people who are agender do not feel like gender is a strong part of their identity, or do not identify with the concept of gender at all.

**Autigender** – for people who are autigender their gender identity is strongly related to their autistic identity. Autism is a neurotype, and some people feel that this has shaped their gender identity so much that they are hard to separate. Only autistic people can identify as autigender.

**Brotherboy/sistergirl** – these are transgender identities exclusive to First Nations cultures in Australia. A brotherboy is a transgender male, and a sistergirl is a transgender female. Many indigenous cultures across the world have their own trans and non-binary gender identities.

**Cisgender** – this simply means a person who identifies as the sex they were assigned at birth. It is from a Latin word meaning 'on the same side as'. It is not an insult.

**Coming out** – coming out means telling others in your life about your gender identity and/or sexuality. People you might come out to include your family members, friends, teachers, employer (if you have one) or health professionals.

**Demigender** – people who are demigender feel a little bit, but not fully, like one of the binary genders of male and female. For example, someone who is a demiboy might feel a little like a boy, but not fully. A demigirl will feel a little like a girl, but not fully. You could put the prefix demi- in front of any other gender-identity label if you feel a bit like it, e.g. demi-agender, demi-genderfluid.

**Family of choice** – people who are not part of a person's biological family but who are close in the way members of biological families are expected to be. Many trans and gender-divergent people select friends as their family of choice when their own biological families treat them poorly or reject them due to their gender identity.

**Gender diversity** – the concept that everyone has a different gender identity. Gender diversity means that there are many more than two genders in the world.

**Gender dysphoria** – gender dysphoria is the distress a person feels due to a mismatch between their gender identity and their sex assigned at birth. Many but not all transgender people experience gender dysphoria.

**Genderfluid** – the gender identity of a person who is genderfluid changes regularly. It could change between binary identities or between any range of other gender identities.

**Non-binary** – non-binary people do not identify as binary male or female. There are a lot of different non-binary identities. Non-binary people may identify as additional identities, such as transgender or demi-gender.

**Pronouns** – a word used to describe somebody other than using their name, such as he/him/his, she/her/hers, they/them/theirs, xe/xem/xeirs.

**Trans/transgender** – a person who does not identify with the sex they were assigned at birth. Transgender people can identify as male or female or something else.

**Trans man/trans masculine** – a transgender person who transitions from female to male and identifies as male and/or masculine.

**Transphobia** – transphobia is hatred, bigotry or trolling against trans and gender-divergent people.

**Trans woman/trans feminine** – a transgender person who transitions from male to female and identifies as female and/or feminine.

**Two-spirit** – 'two-spirit' refers to a person who identifies as having both a masculine and a feminine spirit and is used by some American First Nations people to describe their sexual, gender and/or spiritual identity.

# Youth LGBTQ support organizations

## USA

### Gay, Lesbian, Bisexual and Transgender (GLBT) National Help Center

Toll-free: (888) 843-4564
Toll-free: (800) 246-PRIDE (1-800-246-7743)
Email: help@GLBThotline.org
www.glbthotline.org

The GLBT National Help Center provides peer support, community connections and resource information to people with questions regarding sexual orientation and/or gender identity via the GLBT National Hotline and the GLBT National Youth Talkline and online chat services.

# Gender Spectrum

Phone: (510) 788-4412
Email: info@genderspectrum.org
www.genderspectrum.org
www.genderspectrum.org/about/contact

Gender Spectrum provides education, training and support to help create a gender-sensitive and inclusive environment for all children and teens. Gender Spectrum also offers a wide range of resources, training and consultation to support schools to be more welcoming for all students, regardless of their gender identity.

# The Trevor Project

Toll-free: (866) 488-7386
Email: info@thetrevorproject.org
www.thetrevorproject.org

The Trevor Project provides crisis intervention and suicide-prevention services to young LGBTQ people under 25.

# Trans Youth Equality Foundation (TYEF)

Phone: (207) 478-4087
Email: contact@transyouthequality.org
www.transyouthequality.org

Trans Youth Equality Foundation, a national 501(c)(3) non-profit foundation, that provides education, advocacy and support for transgender children, youth and their families. TYEF advocates for transgender, gender non-conforming and intersex youth ages 2–18.

# UNITED KINGDOM

## AKT.co.uk

www.akt.org.uk

AKT supports young people into safe homes and employment, education or training in a welcoming and open environment that celebrates LGBTQ+ identities.

# Mosaic Trust

www.mosaictrust.org.uk

Mosaic Trust runs programmes for LGBTQ youth.

# Mermaids UK

www.mermaids.org.uk

Mermaids UK supports gender-diverse young people and families.

# Stonewall UK

Information service freephone: 0800 0502020
www.stonewall.org.uk/help-and-advice

Stonewall UK provides information and support for LGBT communities and their allies.

# Switchboard

www.switchboard.org.uk

Switchboard is a charity for LGBTQ people looking for a sense of community, support or information.

# Index

# The Autism and Neurodiversity Self Advocacy Handbook

## Developing the Skills to Determine Your Own Future

*Barb Cook and Yenn Purkis*

£14.99 | $19.95 | PB | 176PP |
ISBN 978 1 78775 575 8|
eISBN 978 1 78775 576 5

Being autistic, you might come across more challenges than others around you, such as dealing with ableism, discrimination in employment or difficulties in your relationships.

Written by two autistic activists, this book will give you the tools and strategies to advocate for yourself in any situation. It covers specific scenarios including work, school, and family and relationships, as well as looking at advocacy for the wider community, whether that's through social media, presentations or writing. Additionally, the book provides advice on building independence, developing your skills, standing up for others and resolving conflict. The authors explore the overall impact of self-advocacy in all areas of your life, building a sense of confidence, resilience and control. Drawing on the authors' extensive experience, this book will help you to successfully prioritize your needs and rights, challenge what is unfair or unjust and make your voice heard.

**Yenn Purkis** is autistic and non-binary and has published a range of books with JKP since 2006. They actively speak at autism conferences and have increasingly spoken and written on autism and LGBTQ+ identities and received the ACT Volunteer of the Year award for work in autism advocacy. Yenn lives in Canberra, Australia.

**Barb Cook** is a Neurodivergent Developmental Educator and holds a Master of Autism degree from the University of Wollongong. Barb is a prolific writer, speaker and advocate on neurodivergence, and is founder of *Spectrum Women Magazine*, NeuroEmploy and the NeuroDiversity Hub, based in Gympie, Australia.

# The Autistic Trans Guide to Life

*Yenn Purkis and Wenn Lawson*
*Foreword by Dr Emma Goodall*

£14.99 | $19.95 | PB | 208PP |
ISBN 978 1 78775 391 4 |
eISBN 978 1 78775 392 1

This essential survival guide gives autistic trans and/or non-binary adults all the tools and strategies they need to live as their very best self.

Blending personal accounts with evidence-based insights and up-to-date information, and written from a perspective of empowerment and self-acceptance, the book promotes pride, strength and authenticity, covering topics including self-advocacy, mental health and camouflaging and masking as well as key moments in life such as coming out or transitioning socially and/or physically.

Written by two leading autistic trans activists, this book honestly charts what life is like as an autistic trans person and is vital, life-affirming reading.

**Yenn Purkis** is an autistic and non-binary writer and presenter. They received the ACT Volunteer of the Year award for work in autism advocacy. Yenn lives in Canberra, Australia.

**Wenn Lawson** is an autistic trans man, psychologist and researcher. He Co-Chairs the Australian Autism Research Council and is on the Editorial Board for the journal *Autism in Adulthood*. He lives in Victoria, Australia.

## The Awesome Autistic Go-To Guide

### A Practical Handbook for Autistic Teens and Tweens

*Yenn Purkis and Tanya Masterman*
*Illustrated by Glynn Masterman*
*Foreword by Dr Emma Goodall*

£12.99 | $17.95 | PB |112PP |
ISBN 978 1 78775 316 7 |
eISBN 978 1 78775 317 4

This book explores what it feels like to be a young person on the autism spectrum and looks at all the brilliant things autistic people can do. Full of insights about being awesome and autistic, this book celebrates the strengths of autism, and benefits of understanding the world in a different way. It looks at all the reasons being you and thinking differently can be totally awesome! It also has tips for managing tricky situations such as meltdowns, sensory difficulties and anxiety. It includes fun activities and diary pages where you can write your thoughts and feelings to help you concentrate on your strengths and work on your challenges. This book helps you to develop the confidence to be who you are and help you live life with as little stress and anxiety as possible.

**Yenn Purkis** is an autistic and non-binary advocate, author and presenter. Yenn has given a presentation for TEDxCanberra and has been a frequent keynote speaker at autism and disability events for several years. Yenn has a number of awards, including the 2016 ACT Volunteer of the Year award.

**Tanya Masterman** is an autistic parent of an autistic child. She is Canberra Coordinator for Gifted 2E Support Australia (a national support group for twice-exceptional young people) and an events coordinator for Yellow Ladybugs, an organization that supports autistic girls and women.